CHRISTIANITY'S PR PROBLEM & WHAT TO DO ABOUT IT

*A College Professor
Accepts The Challenge*

MARK C. MATTES

Published by:
1517 Publishing
PO Box 54032
Irvine, CA 92619-4032

Publisher's Cataloging-In-Publication Data
(Prepared by Cassidy Cataloguing Services)

Names: Mattes, Mark C., author. | Mattes, Mark C. Law and gospel in action.
Title: Christianity's PR problem and what to do about it : a college professor accepts the challenge / Mark C. Mattes.
Description: Irvine, CA : 1517 Publishing, [2023] | Includes bibliographical references.
Identifiers: ISBN: 978-1-956658-28-6 (paperback) | 978-1-956658-29-3 (ebook)
Subjects: LCSH: Lutheran Church—Apologetic works. | Apologetics. | Evangelistic work. | Lutheran Church—Membership. | Youth—Religious life. | People with social disabilities—Religious life. | Theology. | BISAC: RELIGION / Christian Theology / Apologetics. | RELIGION / Christian Theology / General. | RELIGION / Christianity / Lutheran.
Classification: LCC: BX8065.3 .M38 2023 | DDC: 230.41—dc23

Printed in the United States of America.

Cover art by Zachariah James Stuef.

Contents

Dedication:

This booklet is dedicated to
Carol Marie Mattes, loving wife,
mother, and grandmother,
a faithful disciple of Jesus Christ.

Defending the Faith:
A Case for Apologetics

Greetings! My name is Mark Mattes, and I'm a professor at Grand View University. You'll read below a talk I gave at a Lutheran event, but you don't need to be Lutheran to find value in it. With this booklet, I'm seeking to help all who confess the Christian faith in light of secular challenges. I pray that this booklet will be a blessing to you as it was for the original audience who heard it.

———————

Increasingly, there is a resurgence in evangelism. This passion is not unique to our time. We forget that throughout most of our history in the United States, Lutherans were growing in number. Until very recently, Lutherans increased their membership decade by decade. Sometimes that was due to the fact that in bygone days, Lutherans had big families, but growth in the past was due to more than that. Lutherans were marked by a passion for sharing the gospel. The prevailing model for starting congregations was not hierarchical, top-down, and bureaucratic. Instead, it was congregation-centered. Congregations freely granted time to their pastors, who helped start congregations in neighboring communities wherever there was a call for help. A congregational "to-do list" included starting daughter congregations. Helping to give birth to other congregations was embedded in a congregation's DNA. We cannot underestimate the power within congregations to establish much good in the world—proclaiming the saving word and administering the means of grace but also mentoring children and youth by providing a healthy community and a safe haven for those beset by trials, as well as ministering to the underprivileged.

Peter's Directive and New Contexts

A major difference between today's missionary context and that of yesteryear is the fact that our country is no longer a "Christian nation," as many had billed America. That's not to say that Americans are not religious or spiritual. A majority of Americans claim to believe in God. But today, evangelists encounter more criticisms of the faith than in the past. Chances are you are quite familiar with these criticisms. Here's a list that I bet you've heard before: (1) Christians are hypocrites; (2) Christianity is a crutch; (3) the Bible and science are incompatible; (4) a loving God would never send anyone to hell; (5) evil is incompatible with an all-powerful, all-loving God; (6) I'm not so bad, so how can you say I'm a sinner?; and (7) there are many paths to God, and you need to choose the path that's right for you.

Disciples of Jesus cannot turn a blind eye to these objections. Even if you have not raised these concerns yourself, you may find your own children or grandchildren challenging you with them. We are caught off guard when we do not know our faith well. To truly be conversant in the faith is not only to know the Scriptures and the catechisms inside and out but also to be aware of criticisms of the faith and have thoughtful responses to them. Some people raising these criticisms are insincere. They use them as a defense mechanism in order to minimize the impact of God's claim on their lives. But others are sincere. God comes across as hidden to them—not just that God cannot be seen but that His ways are foreign to them. Like the God-fearers on the fringes of the synagogues Paul preached to, those folks are great prospects for receiving the gospel. They already have a sense of their need. But the degree to which you cannot respond to these folks' sincere objections is the degree to which they will never hear the gospel from you. So Paul calls us to "do your best to present yourself to God as one approved, a worker who has no need to be ashamed, rightly handling the word of truth" (2 Tim. 2:15). Even stronger is Peter's charge: "But in your hearts regard Christ the Lord as holy, always being prepared to make a defense to anyone who asks you for a reason for the hope that is in you; yet do it with gentleness and respect, having a good conscience" (1 Pet. 3:15–16).

The faith of yesteryear could assume a public where people were at least nominal Christians. But in today's world, Christians work beside Hindus, Muslims, and unaffiliated secular men and women. Christians need resources to be able to defend their faith. That's where apologetics comes in. Apologetics means defending your faith. Apologetics does not mean defending God. God does not need your defense. He can take care of

Himself—thank you very much! Instead, apologetics calls us to think about faith—in light of its critics. The Christian faith receives unfair slights, smears, and inaccurate publicity. Should that be surprising? The old Adam and Eve always want to remain in charge of their lives, captains of their own fates. They do not think they need a God. Or, at best, they conceive of some kind of "higher power" that meets their own felt needs. A God who claims sinners totally as His own is a threat to those sinners' autonomy. No wonder Paul said that "the word of the cross is folly to those who are perishing, but to us who are being saved it is the power of God."

Even stronger, Paul elaborates:

Has not God made foolish the wisdom of the world? For since, in the wisdom of God, the world did not know God through wisdom, it pleased God through the folly of what we preach to save those who believe. For Jews demand signs and Greeks seek wisdom, but we preach Christ crucified a stumbling block to Jews and folly to Gentiles, but to those who are called, both Jews and Greeks, Christ the power of God and the wisdom of God. For the foolishness of God is wiser than men,

and the weakness of God is stronger than
men. (1 Cor. 1:18, 21–25)

Argumentation alone will never win someone
to Christ. Instead, to be won to Christ, we must
encounter the Holy Spirit who calls us through
the gospel, enlightens us with His gifts, sanctifies,
and keeps us in the true faith. But argumentation can help undermine those barriers that the
old Adam and Eve erect to protect themselves. It
can set straight the slights, smears, and bad PR
of secularism. While apologetics cannot confirm
the truth of Christian faith beyond a shadow of
a doubt—for in this life, we walk by faith not by
sight (2 Cor. 5:7)—it can reinforce our conviction
that the Christian faith offers a deeply satisfying
approach to life (John 10:10) that other religions
and secularism cannot give. The Scriptures unlock
the meaning of the entire history of the cosmos
and humanity as the story of God's self-giving,
sacrificial love, given most clearly in the death
and resurrection of Jesus. Our lives have meaning
when we see ourselves within that story. Outside
that history, it is not clear what our lives would
mean. As Luther put it, God created us just so He
could redeem us. This is the clue to the mystery
of the world. We have a reason to live because,

though sinners, we are beloved of God and we are called to share that love with others.

So the faith is something that we can genuinely commend to our children and grandchildren as well as our neighbors. But we cannot do that if we do not seek to mature in the faith ourselves through the study of the word and its bearing on this world. The faith integrates all aspects of humanity: our heads as well as our hearts and hands. Our hearts are guided to trust in God alone and our hands to reach out as Christ's to serve our neighbor. But Christ's renewing work also includes our heads as we learn to take every thought captive to Christ (2 Cor. 10:5). Apart from apologetics, we are apt to disassociate our hearts and hands from our heads. After all, thinking is really hard work. But disassociation is not Christ's way. He wants to be Lord over the whole person. That new man or woman in Christ sees God's "foolishness" as far wiser than any secular philosophy and God's "weakness" as far stronger than any economic system or worldly power.

One more point: I suspect many of you have felt betrayed by the theology that has paraded itself in the church for the last several decades. One reason for your sense of betrayal is that the church failed to take apologetics seriously. Instead of challenging secular agendas by attempting to see the world through the lens of faith, many theologians adapted or accommodated to this secular agenda and sought some little corner within it where they could still practice some kind of "faith." Rather than challenging critics, these folks internalized secularism and its criticisms so that their faith was watered down and even neutered of its power. But good apologetics leads us in just the opposite direction. While faith in this life can never be proved beyond a shadow of a doubt, it can be defended. Had the church done this, her faith stance would have been clearer, her teachings would have been more solid, and her passion for outreach would have been more vibrant.

My deepest hunch is that the church leadership of a previous generation believed that the wave of the future was to adapt as much as possible to secular perspectives. So pastoral care became like therapy, leadership became like the strategies of CEOs, theology became like secular philosophy, and Bible study became like either antiquarian studies or the self-help section of the local bookstore. We forfeited the very power of God that remakes the world, all so that we might carve for ourselves a little niche in the wider secular public—a venue that itself has no respect for the church and that has many voices working at cross-purposes with the church. Making ourselves akin to another agency of this world, we lose our sense of mission and power. We stagnate. Confessional Lutherans have moved beyond this. In light of apologetics, pastoral care is restored to caring for souls, leadership is resituated as outreach, theology is reseen as the grammar of faith, and Bible study is returned to an encounter with the living God. This is because our defense of the faith means that no more will we attempt to find our niche in a secular world. The secular world does not want us. Instead, we will challenge the most fundamental assumptions of secularism and put them to the test.

The Nature of Secularism

What does it mean to be secular? To be secular means (1) to see life from within the immediate physical and temporal world without reference to God; (2) to establish one's own value system apart from any reference to God, who is only an "external authority"; and (3) to understand that there are no absolutes in life—that all truth is situational. Seeing life as its own end, people seek to find meaning by racking up experiences. Now, we Christians deny all this. But can we prove it wrong? We could if we could find some "bird's-eye view" or independent vantage point from which to argue. That is what the philosophers over the last several centuries have tried to do. But let's be honest: these philosophers have not been successful. But do we Christians have an independent vantage point? Again, let's be honest: no. We offer no truth that anyone outside of Christ could accept. Remember, Paul writes, "For no one can lay a foundation other than that which is laid, which is Jesus Christ" (1 Cor. 3:11). Jesus Christ is our foundation. He is the way, the truth, and the life (John 14:6). Truth relies on doctrines for its expression, but most important, truth is a person, Jesus. He is the measure and fulcrum of truth. Yet no one can come to Him or see this unless called by the Holy Spirit. So we must accept the fact that, for all the things we share in common with non-Christians, our most fundamental view about truth is not shared. How will that shape our apologetics? Very simply, apologetics deals not so much with *arguing people to the faith* as much as *arguing with them from the faith*. In arguing from the faith, we invite nonbelievers to consider what life would be like if they were believers. How would you see the world with Jesus as your Lord?

What difference would it make for your life if the Bible were true?

Faith in Jesus is not shared by all, but there are some things that believers and nonbelievers do share. All people are on the same page when wrestling with life's tough questions, such as: What happens when we die? Does life have a meaning? Is there a God? We all do not share faith in Jesus, but everyone lives by some kind of faith. Again, this is because no one can prove beyond a shadow of a doubt the truth of what one thinks and feels about such questions. So all people are in a sense people of faith—the question is: In what do we, or should we, put our trust?

The Secular Mind:
Running from God's Mercy

Close to five hundred years ago, Martin Luther called for a reformation of the church. He was not the only one to make that call, but no other reformer was as clear as he that what reformation should be about is God's grace offered in Jesus Christ. Late-medieval men and women knew Jesus as a role model for living and as a judge at the end of time, but they did not see Jesus as their redeemer—or at least as clearly as Scripture reveals it. Luther challenged all that and went so far as to base all saving truth on the authority of Scripture. What that means is that Scripture is the prism through which we are to understand God and the world.

Now, the old Adam and Eve do not like grace because it forces them to admit that they need Jesus. Like the first sinners, early modern people were apt to think that any talk of grace undermined their autonomy and agency. So they thought that the answer was to look to reason and not the Bible. Not long after Luther's reform, people sought another basis for truth than that of Scripture. Scripture seemed inadequate to convey truth in comparison with something like reason. Philosophers like René Descartes appealed to reason as the basis for truth, and later philosophers like John Locke appealed to experience. The upshot was that, insofar as it was honored, the Bible was evaluated in light of reason or experience and discarded as the context or prism through which everything else was understood (including reason and experience).

This was the beginning of the secular outlook. These early modern thinkers did not try to get rid of "God," but they reinterpreted God in generic terms as nature's God and the like. Over time, Europeans and some Americans began to feel that if humanity were truly to be set free from the old constraints of the nobility who lorded over peasants and censured free thinking, then that power to which the nobility appealed for their "divine rights," "God," had to be ditched. Their logic was simple: if God has all power, then we have no power. So for us to claim our own power, we must deny God. Some concluded that all "God" ever was is an illusion invented by the powers-that-be to secure their entitlement. The idea of "God" was devised as a ploy or ruse to keep people in line because they would fear God's judgment. Or "God" is merely some kind of crutch to help people cope with the changing shifts of fortune. Humanity becomes more mature to the degree that religion diminishes and is displaced by scientific reasoning. Now, this telling overly simplifies the history of secularism, but there is enough truth in it for our purposes.

Again, most Americans are not atheists. But most Americans see faith as a private matter not bearing on public life. We are inconsistent because we support a "civil religion" with paid military chaplains, chaplains for Congress, "In God We Trust" written on our money, Christmas as a national holiday, and so on. Even so, we undermine the view that faith gives truth. We tend to associate truth with math and science—"verifiable" matters—and religion with subjective feelings. But what really becomes of truth if we unmoor it from God? Can truth survive? In a sense, it does not. Why? Because in the secular perspective, we are *always* skeptical about reality. With such skepticism, all truth ever amounts to is describing what works but not what's real. Thus what used to be truth is reduced to opinion.

Now Christians need to challenge that assumption, if for no other reason than to be true to what science actually does. It's false that religion and science are incompatible. Think: science describes how gravity works, but it is unable to say *why* it should work. We can use mathematics to describe how gravity works, but we are clueless as to *why* mathematics should be successful in describing gravity. Faith alone answers the question of why. It is astonishing how math can be used to measure or map the cosmos in all its dimensions. The mind is quite adept at doing this. But again, why the mind should be so successful in mapping matter is a mystery! That's where faith is all so true to reality and experience. A truly mindful perspective honors this mystery. Such mystery does not stupefy us but instead allows us to enjoy the wonder—even magic—of it all.

Additionally, we need to remind our secular friends that it was Christians who discovered that if you want to understand the world, use math to do it. The master behind all this was a four-teenth-century monk and Oxford scholar, Thomas Bradwardine. Far from being opposed to religion, science as we understand it is one of Christianity's great gifts to the world. But science on its own can only describe physical processes; it has no ability to offer an explanation for them. Because it cannot, a secularistic outlook that attributes truth only to science offers at best only a description of how things work in the world. It dodges the question of *why* things should work the way they do. Such a secular perspective is inherently unsatisfying—at least when compared to the Christian faith, which honors that the mystery behind physical laws is none other than God Himself. God is the mystery of the world who makes sure that we can trust math to decipher physical laws. In so acknowl-edging God, we do not merely support a pragmatic approach to the world—that is, we do not limit our thinking to "what works"—but instead claim to know something about reality. That truth is summarized by the Psalmist: the heavens declare the glory of God and the earth shows forth His handiwork (Ps. 19:1).

But secularism is not just unsatisfying when it comes to truth; it also fails to establish a basis for sound moral discourse. As noted, it proves to be successful in matters of quantification. But unless it smuggles notions of a purpose-filled world or notions of a providential design into public discourse, then modern people have no recourse by which to affirm the freedoms they so cherish. Modern people treasure things like freedom, equality, justice, fairness, and impartiality. But apart from some vision of goodness as such, those words are just fancy abstractions. Critic Stanley Fish notes that "nothing follows from them until we have answered questions like 'fairness in relation to what standard?' or 'equality with respect to what measures?'—for only then will they have content enough to guide deliberation."[1]

We Christians must ask which is more likely: (1) that goodness is a ruse and all that ethics amounts to is "what works" or (2) that such matters accord with nature as God has designed it. True, we cannot prove the latter stance, but unless you are biased against God, it is a more satisfying approach to ethics than the former. At the very least, it is not inconsistent, unlike the former. When my students tell me that ethics are merely expressions of cultural norms and not beholden to universal truths, I catch them off guard. I ask, "If I grade you down just because I do not like you, has anything wrong happened?" These students who were all relativists very quickly become ethical absolutists: "Of course it is wrong to grade someone down just because you do not like them." When I push, asking, "Why?" they explain, "It isn't fair!" I push them even further: fairness is based on a God-given dignity that belongs to all who share in God's own image.

A secular outlook is unsatisfying with respect to not only truth and goodness but also beauty. Whether found in nature, music, or art, beauty is one of God's greatest gifts to us, offering solace, security, excitement, and joy.[2] It is a glimpse into God's intentions for this world. Atheists would have us believe that to be human is simply to be a combination digestive tract and reproductive system that walks. But how totally foreign is that thought to creatures who not only can enjoy beauty but also make beautiful music, art, dance, sport, and theater. If you believe that beauty gives a glimpse into reality, then it's hard to simply believe it is an accident of purposeless evolution. No, instead, it is an imprint of God on nature and expressed, too, in human making and doing. It takes a lot of faith to believe that life is as meaningless as the atheist makes it out to be.

Truth, goodness, and beauty: secularism has a hard time explaining these important matters. But Christians regard truth, goodness, and beauty as names for God, identifying who God is. For that reason, Christians, too, are skeptics. We are skeptical of secularistic skepticism. Belief in God as the Alpha and Omega is a more credible (even if not provable) outlook on life than the thought that everything is due to chance. After all, where did chance come from? For Christians, reason and experience do not float around untethered. They need a context. That's where the Scriptures come in. The Scriptures give insight into how God works with humanity and what humanity owes God and others. Far from constraining human freedom, the gospel liberates people by recognizing that in Christ, we are both lords and servants and that it is wrong to play one over the other. The Scriptures are profoundly satisfying—or as the Psalmist put it: taste and see how gracious the Lord is (Ps. 34:8).

Paul: Master Apologist

Now, here's where apologetics can be handy. Sometimes you cannot prove something beyond a shadow of a doubt, but you can show that the opposing position is empty. That might be the only kind of "proof" that can be afforded in such matters. If your opponent's viewpoints are shown to be inconsistent or unsatisfying, even though you have not proved your position, it is still the one left standing. So if Christian faith accords with reality as best as we can understand it, then something like atheism is ruled out. Indeed, as I hope to show in what follows, being an atheist takes more faith than being a believer because you must explain away so many things that appear to be obviously true.

But I need to mention a caveat: as defenders of the faith, we need humility. Just as in our overall evangelistic program, we are simply beggars showing other beggars where to find bread, so in apologetics we are not to beat people over the head with evidence for the faith. Instead, we are to raise hard questions: Is your secularism really consistent with reality as you believe it to be? Likewise, we need to challenge unfair stereotypes of Christianity that say we are intolerant, close-minded, and unscientific.

The fact that there is no other foundation than that of Jesus Christ does not mean that we are doomed to take a radically relativist stance, where people think, You have your truth and I have my truth. Such an attempt to dismiss truth is bound to fail. Why? You contradict yourself when you suggest that the truth about the one truth is that there is no truth. So let's be honest. Knowledge, accurate information, and reason and logic are still what our brains use to function, but they must function in tandem with experience, wisdom, intuition, values, and faith. Even the scientific method must assume a much wider context than science itself. Again, apologetics calls us to think about the faith. The more we exercise our faith—the more we read the world in light of the Scriptures—the more we deal with unavoidable questions about what reality really is. Christians offer a real service to the world by keeping these questions alive. So the best apologists are ones who really know the Lord and then think about life in light of this knowledge.

We have a model for doing apologetics. It's Paul. Acts 17:16–34 outlines this model. Let's turn to this passage and examine it closely. Note that Paul was evangelizing in Athens, a city known as the center of philosophy. Over four hundred years before Paul, it had been the home to Socrates, Plato, and Aristotle:

"Now while Paul was waiting for them at Athens, his spirit was provoked within him as he saw that the city was full of idols. So he reasoned in the synagogue with the Jews and the devout persons, and in the marketplace every day with those who happened to be there" (Acts 17:17).

Notice the verb *reasoned*. Paul did not just give his testimony. He engaged these people's minds. We need to ask, What would it take for me to do that? When faith is being challenged, we should never be like ostriches and stick our heads in holes to hide from the world. Far too many of us rely on our feelings alone. What we need to do is engage the world with the Scriptures. It is the Scriptures that bring heart, hands, and head together. God has called us to love Him with our heart, soul, reason, and strength. Our sin is that we give short shrift to that third trait—reason—and do not use our heads. Let's love God as God asks of us and start using our brains in our faith walk.

Some of the Epicurean and Stoic philosophers also conversed with him. And some said, "What does this babbler wish to say?" others said, "He seems to be a preacher of foreign divinities"—because he was preaching Jesus and the resurrection. And they took hold of him and brought him to the Areopagus, saying, "May we know what this new teaching is that you are presenting? For you bring some strange things to our ears. We wish to know therefore what these things mean." Now all the Athenians and the foreigners who lived there would spend their time in nothing except telling or hearing something new. (Acts 18:18–21)

Who were the Epicureans and the Stoics? Epicureans taught that the purpose of life is to seek pleasure in moderation. Do what you want, but do nothing to excess. They also taught that there are no gods nor an afterlife. Since there are no gods nor an afterlife, you need not fear death. There will be no judgment. While Paul encountered this group two thousand years ago, it does not sound much different from the secularism I spoke of earlier. "Nothing new under the sun," as the author of Ecclesiastes (1:9) said. We deal today with exactly the same mind-set that Paul dealt with. As was said by Christians in the 1970s, the "new morality" is nothing but the old immorality in a new guise.

The Stoics taught that the soul is a divine spark and that it is on a continuum with "god." The purpose of philosophy is to offer self-help. Their attitude was: Since you cannot change the world—it is far too bureaucratic—you can change yourself by changing your attitudes about life. Again, there is nothing new under the sun.[3] This sounds a whole lot like the self-help section at Barnes and Noble. In fact, it is exactly what would have been called "new age" twenty or so years ago and even today. Where it is similar to Epicureanism is that both schools teach that you are responsible at least for yourself—even though Epicureans see the self as having a lowercase *s* because we are no different from other animals, while Stoics see it as having a capital *S* since our deepest cores are, by nature, one with "god." To the degree that contemporary secularism pushes to affirm that you are the author of your own life—a kind of "god" for yourself—it comes across a whole lot like how many people think today.

Look how Paul got their attention! He earned their belittlement when they called him a babbler. Yet they wanted to hear more! Paul does not run from the name of Jesus but puts it right in front of them. With the resurrection, Paul indicates that we are indeed accountable. The Epicureans and

Stoics are right to affirm human accountability. But they undermine its seriousness because, as Paul points out, we are accountable before God. The resurrection will begin with Christ's coming to judge the "quick and the dead." Then eternal life will begin. More to the point, these philosophers are not totally insincere. We need to learn from that. Yes, Christianity receives some unfair smearing. But not all nonbelievers are insincere. Some are genuinely open to the Christian faith. How's our witness? Do we reinforce non-Christian stereotypes or do we in fact offer a wholesome and grappling witness—like Paul's? Would today's Epicureans and Stoics want to grab you to learn more about the faith?

So Paul, standing in the midst of the Areopagus, said: "Men of Athens, I perceive that in every way you are very religious. For as I passed along, and observed the objects of your worship, I found also an altar with this inscription, 'To the unknown god.' What therefore you worship as unknown, this I proclaim to you. The God who made the world and everything in it, being Lord of heaven and earth, does not live in temples made by man, nor is he served by human hands, as though he needed anything, since he himself gives to all mankind life and breath and everything. And he made from one man every nation of mankind to love on all the face of the earth, having determined allotted periods and the boundaries of their dwelling place that they should seek god, in the hope that they might feel their way toward him and find him. Yet he is actually not far from each one of us, for 'In him we live and move and have our being,' as even some of your own poets have said, 'for we are indeed his offspring.'" (Acts 18:22–28)

The Areopagus was the highest legislative and judicial council of Athens. In a sense, it is like Harvard University and Washington, DC, combined. Here's Paul jumping right in. You and I would at least gulp or even try to run away—but not Paul. What gave him courage? Of course, Christ Himself did. But let's face it: Paul had done his homework too. He did not rely on having been raised in a godly home. Instead, he appropriated that faith for himself. He made it his own. He knew the Scriptures. But read the notes in your ESV (English Standard Version) in the bottom margin. Paul quotes Greek poets and philosophers:

Epimenides of Crete and Aratus. Actually, his overall argument is not so foreign from how early Greek philosophers challenged the traditional Greek gods. For those philosophers, God could not be identified with Zeus, Hera, Poseidon, or Hermes because those gods were unethical—cheating on each other and lying—as well as just too plain human. Paul proclaims that the true God cannot be put into a box—like "temples made by man"—let alone be served by "human hands." The true God cannot be manipulated by us—a scary thought! And yet, this God is unavoidable: in Him we live, move, and have our beings. Again, there's another scary thought, because in light of God's judgment, we are accountable to Him. Paul will not let us off the hook. But see how different he is from a street preacher. He simply states the truth of our accountability; he does not shout, "Turn or burn." What we also can see here is that Paul appeals to the idea that all people have some inkling for God, whether big or small. In our culture, we would call that a "higher power." Again, Paul's point is that whatever we consider "higher" falls short of God. As the Creator of the galaxies, God is always greater. But God is also smaller: God sustains the energy that keeps all the gravity at the core of every atom in place (compare Col. 1:17).

In either case, outside of Jesus Christ, God is a threat to sinners.

> Being then God's offspring we ought not to think that the divine being is like gold or silver or stone, an image formed by the art and imagination of man. The times of ignorance God overlooked, but now he commands all people everywhere to repent, because he has fixed a day on which he will judge the world in righteousness by a man whom he has appointed; and of this he has given assurance to all by raising him from the dead. (Acts 17:29–31)

In light of the proper distinction between law and gospel, one of the most important concerns of Lutherans, Paul is preaching law—calling people to accountability before God. But gospel is implicit: those who repent and believe in that "Man" appointed as judge will find mercy. Paul's word to the Epicureans and Stoics is just as pertinent to today's secularists. Our secularists today want to erase God from public discourse. But they cannot erase some sense of accountability: if not to God, at least to their own senses of integrity. But that is really the gist of it: I'm no sinner because there is no God whose goodness would be the evaluator that condemns me as a sinner. The secularist is trying to justify himself or herself not by faith but (ironically) by unbelief! Erase God and there's no judgment. With no judgment, there's no way I could be deemed a sinner.

But secularists are not so easily let off the hook. Let me explain. The great payoff of not believing in God would be "freedom." Freedom here means that you can invent yourself. Life is one big buffet line of options, and you can take a heap of this or a spoonful of that to make yourself what you want to be. But if we are honest, we have to admit that we do not just make ourselves for ourselves alone. When you make the decisions by which you invent yourself, you are saying that *anyone* could—or perhaps even *should*—live just like you. So you not only invent yourself but, in a sense, invent the world. People who do not want to be atheists but who operate with this outlook end up saying about God, "I determine who God is." If my guilt before God is just too big for me to handle, I do not confess it and get it off my chest through the words of absolution. Instead, I try to reimage a god for myself who is of my "own understanding." And likely this is a god who says, "Boys will be boys" or something like that. We just cannot handle a God who steps right into our own guilt and bears it in His body for us—as Jesus did. If we were to accept that, we would have to admit that we need Jesus. But to do that, we'd have to give up being captains of our own fates. Unfortunately, we never know what it really is to be free—free of having to invent ourselves and be responsible solely for ourselves. Instead, we only have a fake freedom of self-invention.

But let's go back to our atheist. If atheists are really honest about it, they have to admit that they carry the weight of the world on their shoulders. Since they are inventing what is right and wrong, they are a whole lot like Atlas—carrying the entire world—at least insofar as they invent it. That's why the French atheist Jean-Paul Sartre called this responsibility "condemned to be free." Freedom for him means you invent what's right and wrong. Condemned here means that you and everything you deal with are held to this standard you invent. It is an unrelenting standard. There is no absolution for it. There is only the oppressive word of self-evaluation—and evaluation of whatever else that fails to live up to it. So secularist freedom, a "freedom without God," just does not come across as all that positive or good or even free. For atheists, that might be all they have, but a world independent of God's judgment and grace seems to be a world terribly diminished. Back to Paul: "Now when they heard of the resurrection of the dead, some mocked. But others said, 'We will hear you again about this.' So Paul went out from their midst. But some men joined him and believed, among whom also were Dionysius the Areopagite and a woman named Damaris and others with them (Acts 17:32–34)."

What's clear here is that if you are going to be an apologist, you'll need to develop a thick skin. Evangelistic work is not for the weak. It is guaranteed that if you witness, you'll be rejected. Now, many do not like to be rejected. We all like to be accepted. But if you intend to witness to Jesus, you can expect some to reject the message. Rejection is a normal reaction to Jesus. Indeed, it is the *modus operandi* of the old Adam and Eve. It's what put Jesus on the cross. So you already know something about it. But more important is the fact that God's word yielded fruit. Dionysius and Damaris responded to the word. Again, the point is (1) God is calling you to be a witness, (2) God provides a model in Paul, and (3) that model includes an example of defending the faith. The upshot is: get those skills that Paul had to help you defend the faith.

A Lutheran Difference?

Can Lutheranism contribute to apologetics? I think so. Many evangelicals like to marshal as much evidence as possible to support the faith. I do not think that tactic should be avoided. But the Lutheran stance is more apt to unmask secular perspectives as inconsistent or deceptive. Luther was insistent that all people have a "god." This is because the core of being human is your "heart," and the nature of the heart is to trust in something. Genuine faith trusts in God alone and expects nothing but good from Him. But idolatry happens when one's heart looks not to God but instead to some created thing for one's security and good. Instead, one should look to God alone. Luther saw idolatry expressed in the cult of the saints, when people prayed to saints and not God for help. However, even when eschewing God, secularism is its own kind of faith—it has faith in human progress as its alternative to faith in Jesus. We need to drop a Dr. Phil on this perspective: you have a "god"—how is that working for you? Naturally, some are hardened and will not hear of the gospel. But as you read in Acts 17 previously, some will respond. We are too hesitant to ask.

Another way Lutherans can contribute to apologetics is through the theology of the cross. The theology of the cross suspects that people want to be able to bring some quality of their own before God and so earn His favor. That, of course, is the theology of glory. By contrast, the theology of the cross acknowledges that God is at work especially when sinners "utterly despair" of themselves. In no longer looking to one's own resources to secure status before God or whatever "higher power" sinners can muster, we can then actually start to trust in God's love given to us in Jesus. Lutherans believe that God is doing this work of killing off rebellious men and women precisely in order to end rebellion and so open these rebels to receive God's mercy and grace. The theology of the cross recognizes that when people are in a cul-de-sac of their own making, when their own resources fail them, and when they are trapped with "no exit"—and so their defenses go down— then they are receptive to God's mercy. People are not argued into the kingdom. They are open to God's grace when life done on their own terms and in their own ways no longer works.

Finally, Lutherans recognize that God is often hidden, not seen, and not apparent and that His mercy is not always clear. That's why we regularly need preachers to bring us Jesus and His goods of forgiveness, life, and salvation. Jacob wrestled with the hidden God when he wrestled with an unknown opponent in the night. His descendants wrestled with the hidden God when they were in slavery in Egypt and in exile in Babylon. Jesus wrestled with the hidden God when He asked why He was forsaken. Those who struggle with pain and evil in their lives often wrestle with God's hiddenness and wonder when His mercy and healing will appear. Such pain calls for lamentation and even complaint, as we see in the Psalter. Again, we cannot figure out why suffering happens to people who surely do not seem to deserve it. The only thing we can do is uphold them with God's promise that He will surely deliver His people who suffer. Many people critical of faith are in fact struggling with God as hidden, and we need to be pastorally sensitive to them.

Conclusion

In closing, how could we briefly respond to those seven objections to the faith at the beginning of this address? Let's take a moment to look at each. First, *Christians are hypocrites*. True. They are; in fact, everyone is a hypocrite to one degree or another.

Thankfully, you have a Savior who gathers in honest hypocrites like you. Second, *Christianity is a crutch.* But be honest: all people need assistance. At times, life can be unbearable due to fear, guilt, and misfortune. You can be thankful you have a God who keeps His word to sustain you. Third, *the Bible and science are incompatible.* No. Just the opposite—science was birthed in Christian culture and the Bible can provide a context in which the scientific method makes sense. Fourth, *a loving God would never send anyone to hell.* In this life, God's love reaches out to deliver every sinner who trusts in Christ. Those who refuse it must deal with the consequences. So here's the word for you: in your baptism, God has claimed you and promised you a place in His many mansions. Fifth, *evil is incompatible with an all-powerful, all-loving God.* Christians concede that why innocent people suffer and why wicked people prosper in this life is beyond our comprehension. This is a matter that we must hand over into God's care with the conviction that God will manifest His justice and healing in eternity. You are not left to your own devices in facing brokenness and evil, but God has you and these matters well in hand. Sixth, *I'm not a sinner; I'm not so bad.* If you think you need to earn God's approval—better get at it. Let's see how long it takes before you crave God's mercy. If you know you are a sinner, you are exactly at the place where God gives you mercy. Finally, *there are many paths to God, and you need to choose the path that's right for you.* Whether now or later, you will realize that you are not the captain of your fate and that your choices in ultimate matters mean very little. Even worse, it was your rejection of Jesus that put Him on the cross. What counts is that God has chosen you in Jesus Christ so you can enjoy the privilege of living as His child; so repent of your sin, turn to God, and trust in Christ.

God inspires pastors and others to reach out and plant new missions. God, who has imparted this desire, will support us and bring this mission to fruition. As we reach out, apologetics can be our friend. It can help us mature in our faith-walk and help us make the gospel clearer to people. It can help you challenge misunderstandings of the faith and, in so doing, permit faith to germinate in lives far beyond your church doors. May God give us not only the zeal to grow but also the wisdom to share the faith with integrity, maturity, wisdom, and conviction.

Notes

1. Stanley Fish, "Are There Secular Reasons?," February 22, 2010, http://opinionator.blogs.nytimes.com/2010/02/22/are-there-secular-reasons/.

2. See Mark Mattes, *Martin Luther's Theology of Beauty: A Reappraisal* (Grand Rapids, MI: Baker Academic, 2017).

3. Media personality Tim Ferris even promotes Stoicism directly, offering Marcus Aurelius and Epictetus as trustworthy guides to modern life.

Mark Mattes serves as the Lutheran Bible Institute
Chair in Bible and Theology at Grand View
University in Des Moines, Iowa. He is also an
Associate Editor for *Lutheran Quarterly* and
on the Continuation Committee of the
International Luther Congress.

www.ingramcontent.com/pod-product-compliance
Lightning Source LLC
Chambersburg PA
CBHW031259120626
46545CB00007B/2890